Horse Trailer
Owner's Manual

A guide to the preventative maintenance,
repair and safe operation
of horse trailers.

Leigh Goodison Grieve

Sheffield Publications

The Horse Trailer Owner's Manual

Cover design © Leigh Goodison Grieve
www.leighgoodison.com

Technical consultant: David Bodin

Interior art and photos © Leigh Goodison Grieve and David Bodin

Editor: Lizzy Shannon

ISBN-13: 978-0615725734
ISBN-10: 0615725732

Printed and bound in the United States

The Horse Trailer Owner's Manual

A guide to the preventative maintenance,
repair and safe operation
of horse trailers.

Leigh Goodison Grieve

Sheffield Publications

ACKNOWLEDGEMENTS

This book would not have been possible without
the expert assistance, information, guidance, technical
support and encouragement provided by my partner,
David Bodin, "The Horse Trailer Guru."

TABLE OF CONTENTS

Introduction

INTRODUCTION

Far too many horse trailer operators gamble with their lives and those of other motorists by not maintaining, or knowing how to safely tow, a trailer. The purpose of this handbook is to help horse trailer owners and potential buyers, understand how to purchase, maintain, safely operate, and effectively communicate with repair and sales people.

With easy to understand diagrams and explanation of terms, this book should help you make informed decisions about your trailer and safe towing. You'll also learn how to get the most miles out of the trailer you own and what to consider if you're thinking of buying or selling. This handbook also includes maintenance schedules, lists of essential items, handy tips, and troubleshooting help.

"There are no bad horse trailers, there is only bad maintenance."

While competing manufacturers may argue that statement, it is basically fact. Anyone can take a new horse trailer of any make, price, and quality of construction and turn it into a pile of junk rusting in the pasture. Or, they can keep it washed and waxed, properly maintained, protected from the elements, and make it last their riding lifetime. With rare exceptions, the longevity is almost always in the maintenance.

In our current economy, more and more trailer owners are repairing their older trailer rather than buying a new one. There are a number of reasons why this is a good idea. One is that older trailers were built of heavier steel or aluminum than the new trailers.

Current trailer manufacturers will tell you this was to lighten them and thus save on fuel. This is only partly true. Like anything else, it's planned obsolescence (there are many 30+ year old trailers on the road), and they're cheaper and more economical to build. Another reason is that restoring your trailer may cost less than half the price of a new or newer, and often inferior, trailer.

By sharing what we've learned over the years in repairing, restoring and maintaining horse trailers, the indispensable information presented here could save you thousands of dollars in needless repairs. It could also prevent you from buying a lemon, save the lives of you and your horse, or those around you on the road.

Chapter 1

Horse trailer
safety inspections

Horse trailer safety inspections

Over the many years of repairing, maintaining and restoring horse trailers, one indisputable fact became evident. There is a significant lack of maintenance, repair and safe hauling practices on horse trailers. In the states of Washington and Oregon there are no mandatory safety inspections required for trailers. However, there are other states in the U.S. that do require annual safety inspections on horse trailers.

In Virginia (and sources tell me this is true for many of the eastern states), all trailers required to have inspections are those whose actual gross weight (GVWR) is 3,000 pounds or more and required to have brakes. The GVWR is the weight of the trailer plus the weight of any load that the trailer is carrying. If the GVWR is less than 3,000 pounds, it is not required to be inspected; however, any trailer under 3,000 that is equipped with brakes is also required to be inspected. The state inspection fee is $16. The inspection must be performed by a certified, licensed inspector who has passed state requirements. The inspection includes, but is not limited to:

- Pulling off one wheel per brake axle and taking a look at the condition of the brakes, brake magnets, wheel bearings, grease and springs.
- The condition of all tires and their stems, except for the spare.
- All lights and required reflectors, including license plate lights.
- The trailer frame, suspension, and wiring.

- The trailer hitch or coupler.
- The breakaway system, battery and switch.

How does this apply to horse trailer operators in other states? Obviously, if you are traveling to another state it will benefit you to find out what requirements are mandatory in that particular state. Most people are fairly vigilant about complying with equine health requirements such as Coggins tests, vaccines and health inspections before hauling out of state, but they rarely take into account the trailer requirements. In addition, while safety inspections are not currently a legal requirement in our area, they are a good idea. And eventually as other states catch on and realize there's revenue to be had, laws will likely be updated.

Whether or not there are state or federal regulations in place, regular (and by regular they should be at least annual) safety inspections are something you should be having done. With the exception of the wheel bearings (unless you're mechanically inclined), most of the above components are things you can inspect on your own. In addition to the above, you should also be checking:

- Proper and even tire inflation, not only on the trailer but on the tow vehicle as well. The recommended tire pressure is imprinted on the surface wall of the tires.
- Rotted areas or cracks that affect the integrity or strength of the floor.
- Rusted through areas or exposed metal sharp enough to cut yourself or your horse.

- Welds and hinges.
- Any area that wasps can create nests.

Typical places for bees or wasps to nest are in the hollow sections of rear rubber bumpers, along the inside trailer framework and in wiring, in vents, breakaway battery cases and under the trailer tongue. Use extreme caution in routing these pests out, especially if your horse is tied anywhere nearby. The best thing is to wait until early morning or dusk, when they're asleep, then hit them with a wasp spray that shoots a stream from a distance, rather than just a spray.

Even a person who is diligent about trailer maintenance and repair can experience unforeseen problems on the road. Your trailer and tow vehicle should always be well stocked and updated with emergency supplies. Investing in a membership with U.S. Rider is also a good idea as most AAA operators won't haul a horse trailer with live animals. Handy checklists of emergency items and maintenance schedules are included at the end of this book.

Chapter 2

The tow vehicle

The tow vehicle

Whether you already own a tow vehicle prior to buying your trailer, or you plan on buying one later, you should be aware of the tow vehicles capabilities before hauling any load. Many manufacturers ratings state that the vehicle is capable of towing a certain capacity. However, with lighter vehicles, such as SUV's or half-ton trucks, you will be severely stressing all major components (transmission, suspension, brakes, tires) if you exceed the GVWR (gross vehicle weight rating). Exceeding the GVWR can also cause accidents because those components may fail, such as the brakes, which puts everyone at risk. The tow vehicle needs to not only be able to stop itself but also the cargo that it's hauling.

Half ton vehicles and SUVs

A half ton truck, or SUV with the same GVWR, should never be used for towing any horse trailer larger than a two-horse straight load or lighter slant. Nor should they be used to haul a gooseneck trailer as half ton vehicles do not have the suspension capable of handling such a load.

To get a better idea of the capabilities of these vehicles, consider that an average GMC half ton truck has a GVWR of 6450 lbs. If an average two-horse slant tandem axle trailer, unloaded, weighs 3250 lbs, and that gives you a maximum loading capacity of 3200 lbs. Two horses weighing 1000 lbs each take up 2000 lbs, so the rest of your tack and supplies shouldn't exceed 1200 lbs, even if your trailer has a GVWR of 7000 lbs. At that point your trailer weighs more than the tow vehicle.

We've all seen tow vehicles hauling loads heavier than the vehicle, or too heavy for their capabilities. The rear tires are squatted and the front tires are higher, often actually bouncing off the road. When this happens the driver loses his handling abilities and has virtually no steering or brake control. An extremely dangerous situation.

Three-quarter ton trucks

Trucks or SUVs of this size, whether 2 or 4 wheel drive, are suitable for towing gooseneck or fifth wheel trailers, or bumper pull trailers as long as they do not exceed the GVWR of the tow vehicle. Some four horse or trailers with living quarters would need a larger tow vehicle. But again, you need to check the ratings of the tow vehicle and its tire ratings before attempting to haul a larger trailer, especially if it has a load. The tires should be either a D or an E rating to handle the additional load.

When hauling a gooseneck or 5th wheel trailer, the pressure will be forward of the axle and putting the weight on those axles and transferring the weight of the trailer toward the back, so the tow vehicle is not carrying the full weight of the trailer. Generally the hitch on a gooseneck is 5" forward of the rear axle, with the exception of club cab trucks, which may require adapters that will the load directly over the rear axle and not distribute it evenly which can cause problems especially if the tires are not the proper load capacity.

Chapter 3

Hitches, tongue jacks, chains and cables

Load leveling and torsion bars

At the front end of every trailer are a hitch and a jack. There are a variety of hitches for bumper pull trailers, such as the A-frame, which drops directly over the ball hitch, and locks by way of a lever; and the collar lock, which opens like a clamshell, with a collar that slides up and is locked in place with a pin.

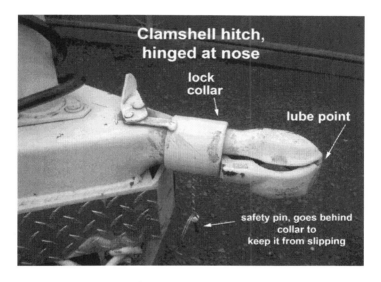

Clamshell hitch, hinged at nose

lock collar

lube point

safety pin, goes behind collar to keep it from slipping

Hitches can be changed according to preference but require welding and possibly expensive modifications. After years of use hitches and receivers can wear out and become dangerous. If the trailer seems to jerk and make a 'thump' when moving forward or stopping, there is now 'slop' in the receiver and/or the hitch that could result in the hitch coming off the ball. These should be carefully measured by a professional using a micrometer caliper to determine if either should be replaced.

It is extremely important always to use the correct size ball for the hitch, but if you tow other trailers with different sized couplers, you may wish to buy a multiple ball mount type of receiver to accommodate both sizes. It is important to also have the mounting system that is usually bolted to the tow vehicle checked for loose bolts that holds them to the framework.

The hidden hitch for gooseneck trailers is popular because it folds over in the truck bed when not being used. Installation involves cutting into the bed of the truck, then bolting the associated hardware and framework into the chassis of the vehicle. As this is getting dangerously close to fuel lines and wiring, you should have a professional familiar with their proper installation install them.

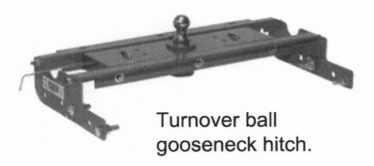

Turnover ball gooseneck hitch.

Trailer jacks are usually the crank system type, but older trailers may have a ratchet style with grease-covered open teeth. These can slip and cause injuries. The size of jack should be a weight appropriate to the size of the trailer, i.e., a trailer rated at 7000 GVWR should have a tongue jack with a minimum 5000 lb capacity. When not in use a 'foot' or a wheel can be inserted at the bottom of the jack. In either case, whenever the trailer is not going to be used, the wheels should be chocked prior to removing it from the tow vehicle.

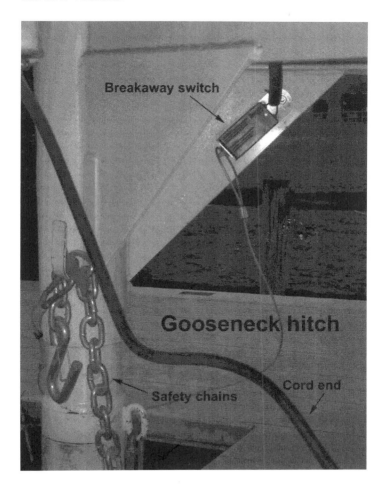

Breakaway switch

Gooseneck hitch

Safety chains

Cord end

An electric jack can make hitching up your trailer effortless.

Electric jacks are available for both bumper pull and gooseneck trailers. These receive their power when they are hooked up to a tow vehicle, via the auxiliary circuit in most cases. A fully charged auxiliary battery can be installed to power electric jacks. They are convenient, though considerably more expensive, and should have a separate charger so as not to drain the vehicle's battery.

Load levelers, or load distribution systems, come in different weight ratings and are part of the hitch receiver and have attachment brackets on the sides of the tongue of the trailer. Their purpose is to take the weight off the rear bumper or hitch receiver of the tow vehicle and transfer the weight evenly across the tow vehicles chassis to evenly distribute the load. These are useful if the tow vehicle is a little on the light side. They are adjustable and help stabilize the trailer as well as act as an anti-sway device in the event that you have to quickly swerve around an obstacle or another vehicle.

Safety chains are required on all trailers. The tensile strength of safety chains should be triple that of the GVWR of the trailer. The end connectors should be the mouse-clip style or screw on, but not just a simple open hook as these can bounce off. As an added safety measure, chains need to be crossed underneath the tongue of the trailer, which will cradle the receiver should it come off the hitch.

Chapter

4

Tow vehicle brakes, trailer brakes and breakaway safety systems

The brake controller

Understanding tow vehicle and trailer brakes is a bit of a mystery. If you have brakes on your tow vehicle, why should you need brakes on your trailer? The tow vehicle slows and so does the trailer. But if you don't have brakes on your trailer, having substantial additional weight pushing your tow vehicle makes it not only more difficult to stop, it increases wear on your tow vehicle brakes. It also increases your stopping distance, depending on road conditions. That's why it is essential to have correctly operating trailer brakes. They put brakes on trailers for a reason.

New, with smooth surfaces Badly worn, deeply scored and unsafe to use

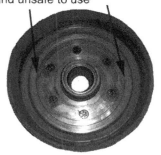

The brake pad and brake magnet surface should be smooth and groove free for brakes to operate properly.

Most new tandem (two) axle trailers have brakes on both front and rear axles. A lot of older trailers (pre 1980's) had brakes on only one axle, either the front or rear. Additional brakes can be installed. Single axle trailers (which are extremely dangerous for any use

other than light utility hauling), don't generally have
any trailer brakes, and are not recommended.

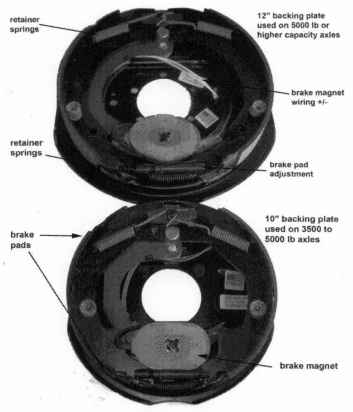

retainer
springs

12" backing plate
used on 5000 lb or
higher capacity axles

brake magnet
wiring +/-

retainer
springs

brake pad
adjustment

10" backing plate
used on 3500 to
5000 lb axles

brake
pads

brake magnet

**Backing Plates: these house all
the brake components**

When the trailer is plugged into the tow vehicle via
the connector, the trailer is now receiving power from

- 34 -

the brake controller in the tow vehicle that signals the brakes to engage when the vehicles brakes are applied. If the trailer is not receiving this power because of a poor connection, the trailer brakes will not engage and you will be relying solely on the vehicles brakes to stop both tow vehicle and trailer.

Bad brake connections can be due to:

- A cord end adapter diluting the signal being sent to the brakes
- Cord end is damaged or corroded inside
- Wiring is cut or damaged
- Bad splicing in the wiring harness
- Worn out controller
- Bad grounding

The brake controller unit that controls the trailer brakes is mounted under the dash of most tow vehicles (unless the tow vehicle came with a factory installed brake controller, which is an option on a lot of newer models). If you don't have a brake control unit, you don't have trailer brakes.

Trailer brakes are adjustable and need to be set up properly so that the brakes neither come on too hard (which will cause the tires to literally freeze up and drag), or too little, so that you are basically relying on the tow vehicle brakes to slow and stop the trailer. Brakes that are set up too high will prematurely wear out the brake pads, and create heat that wears out wheel bearings, spindles, and other mechanisms, including tires and wheel drums. Your electric brakes, for the most part, do not adjust themselves, so it's important that you them adjusted equally and evenly to avoid pulling to the left or right.

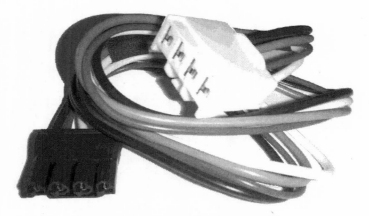

Wiring harness for controller.

There are two ways to connect a brake controller system to the tow vehicle:

- Direct plug-in is the ability to plug directly into the back of the brake controller and into the vehicle's tow package via the fuse block and is designed to work with the tow vehicles computer.

- A traditional brake controller will have four wires extruding from the back and will need to be spliced into the electrical system. These can be complicated and should be installed by a professional in order to work properly.

There are four basic styles of brake controllers:

1. **The timing activated brake controller.**
   These work with your brake switch to activate
   the trailer brakes at a predetermined amperage
   output. It can be mounted from anywhere and
   generally will be used for short hauls, or a low
   weight capacity trailer. Some versions come
   with digital display and direct plug-in capabilities.

2. **The inertia activated brake controller.**
   These controllers function the same way as
   the timing activated with the exception of a
   pendulum sensor. With this style of brake controller the pendulum senses the inertia of the
   vehicle deceleration and proportionally stops
   the vehicle at the same rate. These brake controls have to be mounted to a certain degree
   and they perform the best in areas without
   many inclines and declines. Some models
   come with digital displays and direct plug-in.

3. **The proportional activated brake controller.** Completely redesigned from any previous
   brake controls, the proportional units are fitted
   with accelerometers that measure the g-force
   of the vehicle stopping. These controllers have
   a swift reaction time, the smoothest capable
   stopping, and can handle any trailer in any situation. They can come equipped with digital
   displays, diagnostics, direct plug-in, and self-

adjustment.

4. **The hydraulic over electric controls.** The newest style is the hydraulic over electric controls, which have mini computers that convert hydraulic and brake pedal pressure into electrical current. These controls will be equipped to handle any condition.

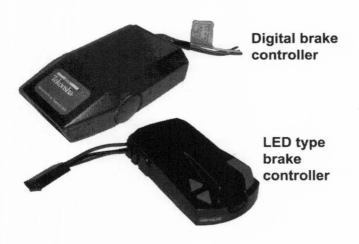

Digital brake controller

LED type brake controller

Now that you understand the brakes on the trailer, there is one more 'last ditch effort' to brake the trailer should the trailer become detached from the tow vehicle: That is the breakaway brake system. The breakaway brake system requires a charged 12-volt battery to function. 12-volt batteries do not recharge themselves UNLESS you have a battery charger installed, which is essential, inexpensive and useful.

The cable and cord end to your brakes acts like an umbilical cord: it is the life support system of the trailer and the brake controller under your dash. But there is always the possibility of the catastrophic situation should the trailer 'leave its mother' and come off the hitch. Should this happen, the breakaway switch cable that is connected to the switch, pulls a pin that allows the battery to send voltage to the brake system and deploys the brakes at full capacity to stop the trailer.

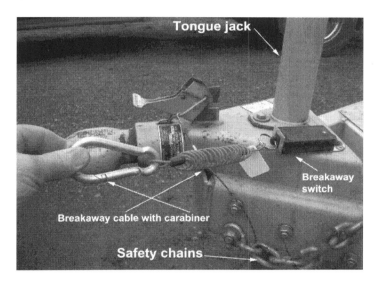

Once the breakaway system is deployed, and it's safe to do so, be sure to chock the wheels of the trailer as the battery charge will deplete and in most cases dissipate within 20-25 minutes, depending on the size of the brakes and how many axles the vehicle has, and the trailer will continue to roll. Remember, you will not have lights, so do not attempt to reconnect the trailer. Instead, when it's safe to do so, chock the wheels, set out reflective devices to warn oncoming traffic, and wait for assistance.

While not all states require a trailer to have a breakaway system, many do, and not having them can result in severe fines. Even if not required, most new trailers are manufactured with them already in place. If your trailer is an older model and doesn't have this system, have one installed. It only makes sense to have that extra measure of security in the case of an emergency.

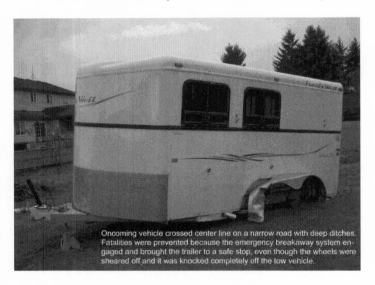

Oncoming vehicle crossed center line on a narrow road with deep ditches. Fatalities were prevented because the emergency breakaway system engaged and brought the trailer to a safe stop, even though the wheels were sheared off and it was knocked completely off the tow vehicle.

If you still have questions about trailer brakes or need information about properly setting your controller, the following are the websites of the most common brake manufacturers:

Tekonsha: 1-888-785-5832 www.tekonsha.com
Hayes: 1-800-892-2676 www.hayesbc.com
Valley: 1-800-344-3230 www.valleytrailerhitch.com
MaxBrake: 1-337-542-4050 www.maxbrake.com

Chapter 5

Wheel bearings, races and seals

Suspension

The suspension, wheel bearings and their components, are very possibly the most important part of your trailer to maintain. If the wheels of your trailer are the legs, then certainly the wheel bearings, spindles and axles are the heart, for without them you don't have a trailer. And while most trailer owners are aware that they should routinely maintain and repack the wheel bearings, unfortunately, this all-important maintenance step is frequently forgotten, or done improperly.

First of all, it's important to understand the wheel bearing system. Each trailer wheel has inner and outer bearings that allow the wheel to spin around the axle with minimum friction. All bearings require lubrication which, if not present, causes the bearing to generate heat. Therefore, it's important to maintain a constant, though not excessive, amount of lubrication as heat can destroy a bearing, spindle and axle. (There are oil bath systems, such as in the Brenderup trailers, but these are not the usual and need maintenance as well.)

A bad bearing can lead to the loss of wheel alignment, uneven and additional wear to your tires, and possible damage to the wheel's rim or your axle. In addition, when the wheel bearings become burned from heat-generated friction, they start to embed bearing material onto the spindle. The spindle is a permanent part of the axle and if it becomes damaged or brittle from heat, it can snap. Having a spindle break is extremely dangerous, not to mention expensive as you have to replace the whole axle. An annual inspection by a professional will determine whether your grease seals are serviceable and have not leaked grease, which can get onto the brake surface. This not only makes the brakes inoperable, but they can catch fire. Grease and rubber are extremely flammable.

·The photo below shows a cutaway of typical trailer bearings, spindle and grease seal assembly.

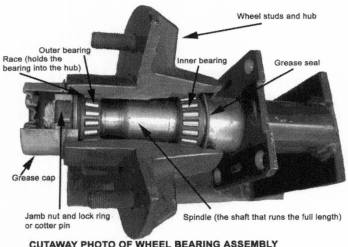

Wheel studs and hub

Outer bearing
Race (holds the
bearing into the hub)

Inner bearing

Grease seal

Grease cap

Jamb nut and lock ring
or cotter pin

Spindle (the shaft that runs the full length)

CUTAWAY PHOTO OF WHEEL BEARING ASSEMBLY

The major problem with the manufacture of horse trailers is that many of the components, especially wheel bearings, are now manufactured in third world countries and the steel is inferior and the parts poorly made. If you've ever bought furniture made overseas, assembled it with the screws that are supplied and they snap the first time you attempt to put the thing together, you'll understand what we mean. These bearings will only hold up for several years; far less if they're not regularly repacked or the trailer is used often. In addition, driving over rough, gravel or pot-holed roads will increase the damage, and unfortunately, these roads are usually how we access our riding trails. The fact is, things wear out, so slow down when driving under these conditions.

So, when you go to your friendly local mechanic and he repacks your wheel bearings, how do you know if he is disassembling them completely, removing the old grease and inspecting the bearings for wear, or just putting new grease over worn and burnt bearings? Or even worse, just pumping the lubricant into the outer bearings without actually removing them? You don't, but these are questions you should ask.

Another problem with trailers is that when they're just sitting unused, and if there isn't much grease remaining in the bearings, without frequent movement the lubricant will eventually settle to the bottom of the bearings and the hub that carries the bearings. When the trailer is finally used again, the top portion of the bearings are devoid of lubrication, so it's 'metal against metal' until the grease heats up enough to partially lubricate the bearings.

Unfortunately, by this time often the metal has already become overheated and damage has been done. Assuming your bearings are in good shape and have sufficient lubrication, take your trailer out for a spin once a month, even if you're not going to ride. This also helps keep the brake surfaces from rusting and avoids surprises in the spring when you're hauling more frequently.

There are a couple of ways you can check for yourself if wheel bearings are becoming worn, even if you have them repacked regularly.

- Take hold of the wheel with the palm of one hand on the inside surface of the top of the tire, and the other hand on the outside surface of the top of the tire, and firmly push and pull with a back and forth motion. There should be a slight amount of play, usually less than an eighth of an inch. Too tight is also not good because this will heat the bearing up. But if you hear 'thunk, thunk,' there is either too much play or the bearing is worn out. Check all the wheels this way.

- After a routine trip when you've been hauling the trailer for at least ten miles, pull over to a safe location and check near the lug nut surface for the bearing cap, where it connects to the hub, for heat. If this surface is too warm to hold in your hand then the bearing is generating excessive heat and may be worn out, have insufficient play or need lubrication. Excessive heat can also be caused by over braking and overloading.

  If you have hub caps or beauty caps, you won't be able to get to those areas so putting your hand on the rim closest to the center will indicate how much heat is being generated. Also listen as you roll forward for any unusual noises coming from the hub cap or bearing cap, which would indicate that the bearing cap has fallen off and is leaking crucial grease. Steam or smoke coming from these surfaces will also indicate a possible serious failure.

The above instructions can be invaluable when purchasing a used trailer, as these are typically the most common and undetected problems that would need attention. They are expensive to repair if the damage is extensive, especially if you break down on a major highway.

Suspension ~~*~~Torsion Axel
Leaf Spring

Your suspension is extremely important, whether you have leaf spring or torsion type axles. Torsions are more maintenance free and do not involve leaf springs, which are on your less expensive trailers. Torsion axles ride better and act like independent suspension.

Trailers with leaf spring suspension have a great deal of moving parts and tend to be on the substandard side from the date of manufacture. Most come with non-greaseable fittings and utilize plastic bushings that are thin, allowing the metal parts to wear out faster.

Upgrade kits are available and well worth the expense. They generally come in a kit to retrofit the existing springs and shackles. Retrofit kits come with grease fittings, brass bushings and are of superior quality to their inferior counterparts. If left unmaintained you could have a catastrophic event, so annual inspection is recommended.

New shackle hangers

Dangerously worn and near failure point

Chapter 6

Trailer tires

Correct tire ratings

Inflation and safety

Tires have an enormous amount of data stamped on the sidewalls, such as the PSI (pound-force per square inch, information for inflating) and date codes. You can also find the date codes by going to the tire manufacturer's website. Date codes are important because occasionally tires are sold that have been sitting in warehouses for years. Rubber deteriorates on older tires, and the ones that have never been inflated have the potential to collapse and come off the rim while traveling.

If you've ever experienced a blow out on a passenger vehicle, you will understand the enormous importance of making sure your trailer tires have been checked for all of the above. This is also one of the reasons we recommend never buying a single axle horse trailer: if a tire was to blow out or an axle break, the trailer could flip over, especially if it only has one horse in it.

- Trailer tires need at least ¼ inch of tread. Check them periodically to make sure they're wearing evenly. Uneven wear indicates over or under inflation or possibly a bent axle, or bad wheel bearings, which will make the trailer appear that it has a bent axle. Tires need to be properly, and equally, inflated. This includes the spare.

- Make certain that your trailer tires have the proper weight rating for a trailer. They should be rated to carry the GVWR (gross vehicle weight rating) of your trailer, which should be listed on the data plate (which is where the VIN is) on the side of the trailer. This is the total maximum weight that the trailer can carry, including its own weight. When you deduct the trailer weight from the GVWR, this will tell you what its load carrying capacity is. The tire rating should be a minimum of load range D or higher.

  Older trailers may not have a data plate but your GVWR is generally on the title or registration. These days, the maximum GVWR is the failure point and the lower you stay under that number, the less wear and tear there will be to the brakes, bearings, etc.

- Tires should be trailer rated with grooves for dispersing water to prevent hydroplaning. Do not use traction type tread which will grab surfaces harder, rather than sliding when braking or pivoting (especially your left rear pivot tire), which is used the most due to it being on the driver's (and most visible) side. Eventually this will prematurely wear out your bearings and suspension.

- Never use light passenger vehicle tires, low-profile, or retreads on a horse trailer. Not even as a spare.

- Never use studded tires or chains on a horse trailer. Chains are intended only for tires that have power supplied to them. If road conditions are bad, either don't go, or pull over and wait until road conditions improve or plan to overnight somewhere.

- If at all possible, have your spare mounted inside the horse trailer. This has three purposes: 1. It will protect it from the elements, especially sun exposure. 2. It prevents it from being stolen or vandalized. 3. On long trips, it is advisable to carry two spares.

- Check your tires regularly for cracks or sun damage.

- Always have wheel chocks, a tire-changing block or jack, and a tire iron in your tack room. It's also a good idea to have an aerosol can of Fix-a-Flat for small punctures.

- Make sure your tires are the same size and rating on all four wheels so as not to cause an imbalance or uneven wear.

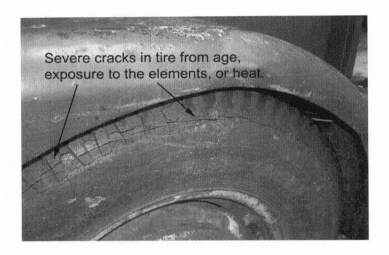
Severe cracks in tire from age, exposure to the elements, or heat.

Chapter
7

Brake circuits, interior and exterior lights

Wiring, auxiliary chargers and customized lighting

The lights and brake system on your trailer operate when they are hooked up to your tow vehicle. If all the wiring and connections are unbroken, clean and properly grounded, then you should be receiving power to your brake system and lights. If any of the systems are not working then you have to look for the problem, which in many cases is just improper grounding, a burned out bulb or a blown fuse in your tow vehicle. However, newer tow vehicles have their own separate fusing system under the hood to feed the trailer.

A broken wire or bad splicing may require a person who is knowledgeable about electrical wiring to track down the problem, which may be hidden in the tubing framework, or underneath the trailer. Another reason for your wiring system not working may be due to the electrolysis that is created from using aluminum rivets to ground the system, which will oxidize and fail. Stainless steel hardware is always preferable.

It is a good idea to carry spare light bulbs for your trailer, as well as spare fuses for your tow vehicle. The correct size of fuse should be listed in the owner's manual for your tow vehicle, or contact a dealership or manufacturer.

The auxiliary lighting system of your trailer should never be hooked up to the breakaway battery. This is for the emergency breakaway brake system only and needs to be maintained for that purpose and that purpose alone! People who utilize their auxiliary battery and or their breakaway battery as a source for supplemental light are setting themselves up for problems because once the battery is discharged it is not capable of energizing the brake system in an emergency situation until it is recharged.

An auxiliary battery that can work your lights when you're not hooked up to a tow vehicle can be installed separate from the emergency breakaway battery system. The auxiliary battery will eventually drain down when used. So it is important to recharge it when you're stationary by plugging it into a charger for that purpose, such as an exterior AC outlet of your house that will maintain it and shut off when fully charged.

If you are not a frequent hauler your battery will not have enough time to charge just by hooking up to your tow vehicle and driving for a few miles once in a while. Another alternative for extended use is to carry a portable gas generator and there are many good, inexpensive units on the market. It will also charge the auxiliary battery.

For people who trailer overnight or under dark conditions, exterior lighting is a must for safety as well as potential theft prevention. A well-lit interior makes it more inviting for loading a horse at night, as few horses wish to venture into a small dark space. More lighting on the exterior makes your trailer a safer place to be and horse will be less anxious as well. Additional exterior floodlights can be installed all around the trailer, including specialized lights with remote control switches. You are then able to turn on the lights from a distance, allowing you to easily

identify your trailer location and warn off anyone
with a mind to breaking in or bad intentions.

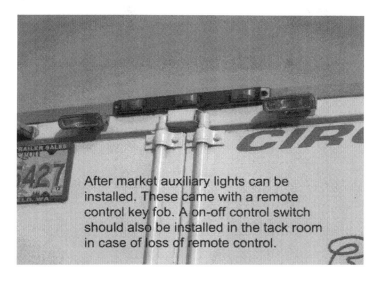

After market auxiliary lights can be
installed. These came with a remote
control key fob. A on-off control switch
should also be installed in the tack room
in case of loss of remote control.

For occasional use inside the tack room or stall area
of the trailer, inexpensive LED lights with magnetic
backs or hooks (for using on an aluminum surface)
are a great way to light up a dark space. If you use
them on the trailer exterior, remember to remove
them before driving off or you will likely lose them
somewhere on the road.

Note: It is important to disconnect the tow vehicle
from the trailer when stationary to prevent the auxiliary battery from draining the battery of the tow vehicle.

Chapter 8

Trailer structure and framework

All trailers begin with a chassis or a frame. The framework for the trailer is then built around the chassis. Before either the steel, aluminum or composite skin goes on, the trailer frame looks much like a Conestoga wagon without the canvas cover. Then the steel or aluminum is welded or pop riveted to the framework and painted. The framework is rarely primed beforehand, and though you'll hear terms like 'electroplated' or 'galvanized' steel, all steel will eventually rust. It is common now to have steel frames with aluminum skins, but if there is no protective barrier between the two dissimilar metals, electrolysis will occur and aluminum will deteriorate and oxidize.

In wet climates, the single biggest problem is with water getting into the framework and being unable to escape. When temperatures drop, the water in the framework freezes and expands, distorting or splitting the metal. With steel trailers, water and freeze damage equals rust. But with both aluminum trailers and steel, the frame will be structurally weakened once it splits. It is also much more expensive to repair, and may require removing the split metal and installation of a new support beam. Many double walled trailers have Styrofoam insulation between the walls to act as an insulator or to reduce sound. However, when water is allowed to ingress the Styrofoam only helps to trap moisture inside.

As with any framework, the more supporting cross members underneath the floors and 'beams' on the upper framework, the stronger the trailer will be.

Cross members on a typical floor should be a minimum of 16" apart, but 18" is acceptable. In the case of a rotten or weak floorboard, the horse is less likely to fall through if the cross members are closer together.

Trailer tongues should always be of a length, weight carrying capacity and strength to safely balance and haul the trailer, livestock and anything else you may pack into it. There are a number of home built trailers on the market that often don't meet even the NATM (National Association of Trailer Manufacturers) standards, which, if the manufacturer is a member, has a sticker that states 'trailer must meet minimum safety standards.' What is considered 'minimum safety' is frightening enough, but when 'backyard trailer builders' don't even need to follow those standards, it's dangerous for everyone on the road.

The length of a trailer tongue, and position of the axles, will determine how quickly it pivots when turning. The tongue length should be appropriate to the length of the trailer. This is not usually a problem with commercial manufacturer's models, but as in the case with home built trailers, again, improper engineering and a shorter tongue will bow the tongue and distort the main framework and sheet metal. A longer tongue gives a wider turning radius and is less likely to jack knife the trailer. They are also better if you have a camper on the back of your truck that extends over the rear bumper. We've all seen trailers with dented noses from turning too sharply. This is either from having too short a tongue or an improper hitch extension that give more clearance between the tow vehicle and trailer, especially when using campers.

Horse owners who travel with their horses will often buy factory installed hay racks or have them installed after market. Hay racks cause more problems than they solve. Unfortunately, most trailers are not manufactured with the structural strength on the roof to carry the weight of hundreds of pounds of hay. If not properly installed by anchoring the rack into the framework, they will damage the interior and exterior of the trailer. Any holes drilled need to be properly sealed to ensure the roof won't leak. This is also true for ladders accessing the roof.

Additional weight added to the trailer, be it any accessory or gear, installed after the trailer was manufactured will exceed the overall GVWR limits.

Take into consideration your additional weight when climbing on the roof. If you do have a hay rack, at least displace the weight with a platform so you don't dent the roof of the trailer. Standing on the roof will also break the seams, and cause the roof to leak and rust.

Chapter 9

Roof, windows and vents

Eliminating leaks

Most horse trailers, aluminum, steel or fiberglass, will eventually leak no matter how well you maintain them or keep them under cover. Aluminum flexes more than steel, which puts stress on seams, welds, and pop rivets, and deteriorates the pop rivets holding sheet metal onto the frame. If aluminum trailers are acid washed, the acid eats away the caulking and allows water to get in.

Ways to prevent leaks:

100% Silver marine grade (handwritten annotation)

- Never walk on the roof or place anything on it without the roof framework first being structurally prepared for such weight
- Make sure there is no rust between roof seams and the caulking is not dried out or missing
- Make sure vents are closed during bad weather, that they fit properly and caulking is in good shape. If necessary, use 100% silicone or a marine grade caulking to repair.
- Check for missing rivets, cracks or holes by placing a bright light on the inside of the trailer at night, then go outside to see where light is shining through

When the caulking deteriorates on a steel trailer, dirt and water get trapped in between the seams. If the trailer is stored under trees or in a dark area, moss may grow, which in turn holds more water. Once the seams begin to rust, any rust, old caulking, flaking paint or moss must be completely removed and the steel treated with a rust inhibitor, cleaned, reprimed and repainted before reapplying caulking. Old caulking on aluminum trailers also needs to be removed and the surfaces properly prepared before applying new.

If you are getting leaks from around the vents it may be that the seals, if they are present, or the caulking, has dried out or deteriorated. Or the vents may be so rusted they don't shut properly and need to be replaced completely. Never travel with your vents open forward as this not only forces water into the stall area, it also creates wind noise that may upset the horses. When vents are open facing to the rear, the hot air generated by the horse's body is able to escape as hot air rises.

Deteriorated window seals, misaligned windows or open sided stock trailers will let moisture in. Removable Plexiglas sliders can be custom fitted into stock trailers but these are by no means waterproof. They will also reduce the amount of ventilation in the trailer if there are no roof vents, so take into consideration the extra heat generated by horses, especially during summer weather.

Fiberglass roofs are not immune to the elements. A good quality fiberglass conditioner/wax should be applied frequently or on an as-needed basis after cleaning thoroughly. Fractures or spider web type cracks should be treated and/or repaired before applying the conditioner. You may need multiple coats to restore the condition of the fiberglass. If it becomes too brittle it will eventually fracture and replacement may be extremely expensive if not impossible with an older trailer.

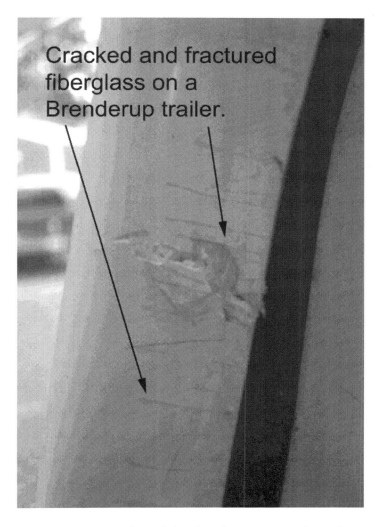

Cracked and fractured fiberglass on a Brenderup trailer.

If you have a steel roof that has become too dented and misshaped to create a good seal with caulking, it may be necessary to apply a rubberized membrane coating. This essentially seals off any exterior moisture. But again, before applying any exterior coating, the surface needs to be impeccably clean, all rust and old caulking removed, and a rust-inhibiting primer and paint applied.

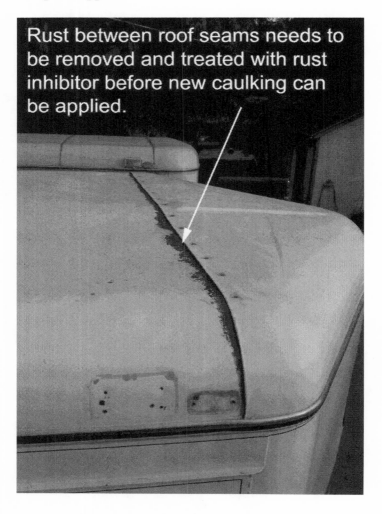

Rust between roof seams needs to be removed and treated with rust inhibitor before new caulking can be applied.

After parking your trailer and chocking the wheels front and rear, the trailer nose should be elevated six inches to allow excess water runoff.

If you can't keep your trailer under cover, you should invest in a trailer cover such as those manufactured by Beverly Bay (www.beverlybay.com) Although these can be cumbersome to put on, there are tricks to make it easier. Roll the cover up like a sleeping bag. Then place a sturdy stepladder at the rear of the trailer and have a helper hand you the rolled up cover. Place it on the trailer roof and unfurl it so that it rolls toward the front of the trailer. You will then be able to drop down the front and sides of the cover until the trailer is covered, then secure the ties.

If you are can't afford a cover, a tarp tied down securely will help keep the water off your roof and from getting inside. Just remember to check occasionally for tears in the tarp, and condensation or mildew that might be forming underneath. Whenever your trailer is covered, or not being used, it's always a good idea to have a portable dehumidifier such as the Eva-Dry 500 or the similar Remington unit, to help reduce moisture inside. Do not use 'disposable' dehumidifiers because it's too easy to forget to replace or empty them. When the moisture evaporates, the dissipating chemicals coat the inside of the trailer and your tack with toxic acidic residue that can cause corrosion and be potentially harmful to humans and animals. If you're not using the trailer, it's a good idea to remove the tack during wet or extremely hot weather.

Chapter 10

Care of paint and aluminum surfaces

Painting a horse trailer is different from any other kind of paint project. The preparation work is 99% of the paint job and it is labor intensive, slow and expensive. Anyone can spray paint on a rusty trailer, but like an apple that is rotten at the core, it will continue to deteriorate from the inside out. And soon, not only will that new paint job be covered with streams of rusty bleeding, the metal continues to rust (or cancer as we aptly refer to it) from the inside out.

The only way to repair the trailer and perform a paint job that will last so it won't rust further, is to remove all the rusted steel or preferably sandblast the existing framework down to bare metal. This will entail removing all the trim, lights, etc., then prime, seal, and repaint with a marine grade epoxy primer and sealer, before repainting.

Even at the manufacturing stage, new trailers rarely have primer put on before painting. You'll hear fancy terms like 'electroplated steel,' but the bottom line is that if they don't have a coat of primer underneath the paint the way automobiles do, the paint will eventually just blister and flake away.

Customers frequently call and ask for a 'ballpark figure' on a paint quote. Unfortunately, that request is almost impossible because every trailer manifests rust and other damages in different ways, due to the way they've been stored, used or maintained. Therefore, each one of them has issues pertinent to them and even a complete inspection will only allow us to ascertain the exterior surface. Until plywood or rubber matting on the walls is removed, taken the aluminum trim off the outside, or the rubber or aluminum trim from around the windows, we can only guess from experience as to how much rust lurks underneath.

So, is it worth it to repaint your trailer? Ask yourself:

- Do I want my trailer back, good as new?
- Does it serve my needs?
- Is there nothing (major, i.e., shape/size/model) I'd change on it?
- Would I prefer a newer model trailer?

Answering these questions (along with a fairly substantial investment), determines whether or not to restore and repaint a trailer.

Is the investment to restore and repaint worth it? It can be. While you will rarely recoup your investment, new trailers, unless properly stored and maintained, will deteriorate just like the older ones. The difference is that most (steel) trailers manufactured after the mid 1990's are made with a much thinner gauge of steel, and we are seeing even three to five year old trailers that have rusted worse than the older ones. To restore and repaint on a typical two horse straight load or slant, bumper pull, you will probably spend about half the price of what a new trailer would cost.

Even at that, new or old, restored or living with what you have, maintenance is everything. If you can store your trailer or keep it covered during wet, cold months or even hot dry ones where the sun oxidizes the paint and deteriorates rubber, you are money ahead. *Do not acid wash!*

Aluminum trailer exteriors are not maintenance free. Painted aluminum should be treated like paint on steel trailers—wash with a mild solution of Dawn dishwashing liquid in five gallons of water, and wax periodically to maintain. However, with bare aluminum, many people turn to the 'quick fix' and take it to a truck stop to have it acid washed. Acid washing aluminum removes some oxidization, but this is temporary and will return in several months. And acid washing will never give it back the original shine. In the meantime, what the acid washing has also done is eaten away the caulking and stripped the aluminum of its natural protective qualities. You should never power wash a trailer as this will strip off paint as well as caulking. *Do not pressure wash!*

Acid washing is a 'quick fix.' If you want your aluminum trailer (or any aluminum surface, such as diamond plate trim) to shine, you need to remove the oxidization, polish the aluminum and seal it so it will stay shiny for longer. Of course, this is a much more labor intensive process.

To remove the oxidization from aluminum, apply a good quality aluminum cleaner with #0000 steel wool (or #000 if heavily oxidized; too coarse a grade, such as #00 will scratch the aluminum). Allow the black oxidization to come to the surface, wipe off, then buff to a high shine. Again, heavily oxidized, or pitted aluminum may take several applications to achieve the desired results. You can't remove the pitting from aluminum or diamond plate trim, but having mud flaps on your tow vehicle will help prevent damage from rock chips. Aluminum polishing is best left to a professional.

Chapter 11

Buying a horse trailer: new or used

What you need to know before you start shopping

Before you start shopping for a horse trailer, whether you've owned one previously, or this is your first, there are several important factors to take into consideration:

1. Your budget
2. Your tow vehicle
3. Your needs
4. Your horse(s) needs

If you are buying a new, lower end trailer, be prepared to pay for options that in the past were standard. These can include rubber matting on side walls, rubber mats on the floors, and even the spare tire. While there are some items that you may think you can add later, it's usually less expensive to have them installed at the time of purchase. The other thing to check for on a new trailer is quality of workmanship: door alignment, enough door support hinges, or any sharp, unfinished metal edges that might cut your horse.

GVWR

A three horse trailer with tack, supplies and horses could add up to 3500 lbs or more, so you should check the GVWR of the axles. If there are two 3500 lb axles, that's only 7000 lbs of carrying capacity. If the trailer weights 3500 lbs and your cargo is at 3500 lbs, you are at your maximum capacity, and overloading is not only dangerous, it prematurely wears out brakes, wheel bearings and other important components.

Purchasing a good quality used trailer can be a great alternative, but there currently are no Lemon Laws on horse trailers. If you find you've bought a trailer that is unsafe and requires more work than it's worth to get it running, you'll be stuck with it. You should also be familiar with the major operating components of a horse trailer, and what to look for in the way of maintenance that may or may not have been per-formed, as few people keep service records the way they do with motorized vehicles.

If you don't own a vehicle with the GVWR capabili-ties for towing a horse trailer, you should shop for that first. It's far better to have more towing capacity than less. Half ton trucks or tow vehicles are limited in towing capacity and even with tow packages, should only be used for two horse straight loads, or light two horse, slant bumper pull trailers. They are not suitable for towing any size of gooseneck trailer. A vehicle towing a trailer that exceeds its tow capaci-ty is going to cause excessive and premature wear and tear on the transmission, suspension, and tires.

Occasionally riders consider buying more horse trail-er than they will use because they plan on hauling friends' horses. Larger trailers require larger tow ve-hicles that in turn consume more fuel and they are more difficult to turn around in tight spots. Hauling friends' horses can be problematic if their horse has hauling issues, or the friend is not forthcoming about sharing costs for maintenance or fuel. In addition, loaning a trailer can have ramifications if damages occur, i.e., who is responsible for paying, or if insurance company will cover it. Many a good friendship has been lost because of misunderstandings with sharing of a horse trailer.

You should also take into consideration what accoutrements you need, would like to have, or could live without. If you plan to horse camp or stay overnight in your trailer, you don't necessarily need to have living quarters. A large enough tack room to lay out a cot for sleeping, an adequate tack room for a water tank and your personal supplies and tack is a basic requirement. Upgrades and customizing comes at a price, but again, it's often less expensive to acquire at the time of purchase, rather than later on.

It's rather curious that while many riders are buying bigger horses, such as Warmbloods, Friesians, and other large breeds, trailer manufacturers appear to be downsizing. A true Warmblood sized trailer is 7'2" tall and 8' wide. It's extremely important that you measure your horse BEFORE you buy the trailer to make certain it will fit comfortably. An uncomfortable horse can damage the trailer and harm himself if he feels claustrophobic. Measure not only his height and width, but his entire length from nose to tail then take these measurements with you when viewing the trailer. If he won't fit comfortably (either in a straight load or slant), then don't consider buying as you won't be able to return it.

The most important thing to do before buying a horse trailer, whether it's new or used, is to first **measure your horse,** from:

- the withers to the ground
- the poll to the ground
- muzzle to tail
- the horse's width

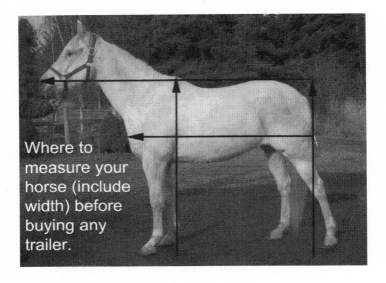

Where to measure your horse (include width) before buying any trailer.

If you are considering a straight load, also measure from chest to tail. If you've owned a trailer before you probably know what make and style works best for you and your horse. Just bear in mind that manufacturing standards have changed over the years. A measuring stick with a level to measure the height is the best choice because a tape that curves around the horse's body will give you a false reading.

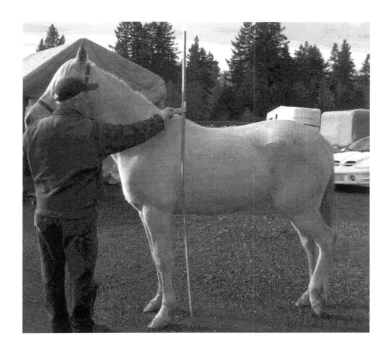

Most straight load trailers built before the 1980's were considerably smaller than the ones manufactured in the 80's-90's. Unless the trailer is a true warmblood size, or ordered extra tall or wide, manufacturers appear to be downsizing again and many of the new slant loads are not very large. While this might not seem to be an issue, small breeds such as short-backed Arabians and ponies, are having difficulty fitting on the diagonal in new slants. This is resulting in behavior problems when hauling, as well as extensive damage to the trailer by an unhappy horse. In most states there are no Lemon Laws on horse trailers, so if you experience buyer's remorse there is little recourse open to you.

Determine beforehand:

- What size of trailer (height, capacity) you want vs. need
- Do you have an appropriate sized vehicle with towing capabilities
- A brake control unit in your tow rig
- Is the vehicle capable of having a brake controller installed
- If your horse is going to fit comfortably in the trailer you're considering

Buying new

The old adage, 'you get what you pay for,' also holds true with horse trailers. If a new trailer is cheap, so will be the trailer. Be prepared to have to pay for a lot of 'options,' which could be anything from rubber mats to a spare tire. Warranties are only as good for as long as the manufacturer stays in business and generally have a lot of fine print, so are not worth taking into account when purchasing.

Buying used

The variables on buying used trailers are so great we could not cover them all in a single column. Maintenance is everything. If you can verify that a used trailer has been maintained the way we've talked about in the previous chapters, then you are money ahead in purchasing a good, used one. On the other hand, purchasing a used trailer that requires several thousand dollars in repairs before it is safe and usable, is worth considering if the seller will take into account what repairs are necessary and adjust their price accordingly.

Straight load vs slant

Although the preference these days is with slant trailers, consider that a side to side rocking motion at a 45 degree angle is not a natural movement for a horse. A horse stops and starts comfortably with forward and backward motion. While there are a lot of experts who may claim that horses ride more comfortably in slants, the majority of trailers with horse-inflicted damage are slants, not straight loads. The exception to this is the horse that will scramble into a manger. If your horse will only haul in one type of trailer, we suggest that you train it to haul in various scenarios, especially if getting out of a bad situation meant the only way out was in an unfamiliar trailer set up.

Aluminum vs. steel

Aluminum trailers first became popular when gas prices began to rise. We were told they were lighter and therefore our towing rig would use less gas. However, in order to make the aluminum as strong as steel, more material needs to go into the trailer, thus making the fully aluminum trailer heavier.

Steel framed trailers with aluminum skin have become popular for the same reason, as well as addressing rust issues in wet climates. However, the aluminum that is being used is so thin that it would not withstand a significant enough impact to protect the horse.

It's extremely important to understand the manufacturing specifications on a new trailer before making the investment. Don't just take a salesman's word for the safety and stability—do comparative studies so you know what exactly it is you're paying for. A lot of trailer salespeople are not horse owners or horse savvy and are not always knowledgeable on the subject.

Ramp vs. step up

While this is a personal preference (and goes along with 'my horse won't load…' etc.), again, it's also about training. The problem with ramps is that they eventually become bowed from the horse's weight, hinges rust and fail, and they become an expensive fix. Some trailers appear to have a step up too high for a horse, but a horse can be trained to back out of just about anything. Consider carefully whether you really need one.

Basic steps when considering a used horse trailer:

Ask about the maintenance done (i.e., when wheel bearing repacks were last repacked.) Most trailers come with third world country wheel bearings when they're manufactured. This steel is extremely inferior and the bearings are usually only good for a few years, at best, but mostly they have to be replaced, even if the trailer is almost new. It's expensive to replace them, but if they're let go they will eventually embed bearing material onto the spindle, which will score the spindles. If the spindles have to be replaced it's a much more expensive fix as they're part of the axles.

How frequently it was used. No use at all can be worse than regularly towed. When trailers sit for long periods the wheel drums and brakes can get rusty and cease up, and the grease in the wheel bearings deteriorates from lack of use and if there's not much of it, will settle. Then when it gets hauled again it's steel against steel (causing friction and unnecessary wear) until the grease heats up enough to lubricate.

Peel back the floor mats and check the wood for rot or splits; with aluminum floors check for pitting and corrosion. Keep in mind most wood floors, from the manufacturer, are not of high quality lumber.

Check for kick marks on the rubber mats inside and if they go through to the outside walls.

If a trailer has a water tank, these usually end up leaking because people forget to winterize or drain them. Check the carpeted area around it to see if there are any water stains. Again, if they're wood floors underneath the tack area, leaking water will have gotten into the wood and deteriorated it. So be careful there and don't forget to look underneath the floor as there is generally no undercoating or protection present.

Look at the roof and check the caulking (for drying,

pulling apart at seams, etc.), especially with aluminum trailers that may have been acid washed.

Check tires for even wear on the treads to rule out anything like a bent axle. The tires should be evenly inflated to manufacturer's specifications.

Ask if you can take it for a road test, which will allow you to see if the lights and brakes work.

Listen for loose suspension or unusual noises, such as broken welds.

Chapter 12

Winterizing
the trailer

Preparing your trailer for winter

When people start thinking about getting a trailer ready for winter, many assume it's only RVs, travel trailers or horse trailers with living quarters (LQs) that need extra preparation. This is not true. You can extend the life of any trailer with taking a few precautionary steps.

The biggest enemy of trailers is exposure to the elements. During the summer it's the sun oxidizing the paint, deteriorating rubber and drying out caulking. In the winter, at least in the Pacific Northwest, if your caulking is missing or shrunk away, rain and condensation leak into the stall and tack areas, causing mold and mildew. Any dirt that is trapped along trim will gather moss and lichen, especially in the areas you can't see, such as on the roof.

It's important to prepare your trailer for winter whether you continue to use it several times a week or stow it away from November until spring riding weather. Let's start with the basics:

Give the trailer a good washing using Dawn dish soap, warm water and an RV brush. You should also have a couple of small, soft bristled brushes, such as toothbrushes or Dollar Store types. Clean the trailer thoroughly, using the toothbrushes for trim lines, around diamond plate and windows. Don't forget to clean that roof, but NEVER walk on it as you will split seams and cave it in! If stubborn stains persist, use a small amount of Comet on the end of a toothbrush. The bleach in the Comet helps prevent new mold from growing. Be smart and safe, using a sturdy ladder and an extended brush. Make sure you rinse thoroughly.

Once the trailer is dry, you should give it a good waxing, which will also help repel water. Then inspect the caulking on the roof and seams. If it appears to have shrunken back or is missing, have this repaired or do it yourself using a 100% silicone or marine oil-based caulking. If you're not an expert at caulking you can get into a mess really fast, so you should know what you're doing.

Freezing winters

During wet winters, rain and condensation will eventually find its way into the tubing framework (steel or aluminum). If the water has no means to escape, when freezing temperatures occur, this water will expand and burst the metal. The only way to avoid this is to provide drain holes to allow the water to get out. Drill a small 3/16 inch hole where the tubing dead ends. This is usually better left to a professional. With double walled trailers it can be difficult to know where to drill without knowing the structure. If your steel trailer has never had drain holes, black or rusty water may leak out for quite a while. Once all the water has escaped, wash it away, then remove the bleed with a cleaner wax and a Mr. Clean Magic Eraser. Stubborn rust can be removed with a small amount of Comet, rinsing thoroughly afterward and reapplying wax. Drain holes must be kept free of scale.

Drill h2o escape hole

Obviously, trailers that are stored under cover will last the longest. Trailer paint, always substandard at best, will also fare better. Most people don't have this luxury, so the next best thing is to invest in a trailer cover, such as those sold by Beverlybay.com. Even a tarp is better than nothing. Just make sure to secure it so it doesn't flap or trap the rain underneath.

Now that your trailer is dry on the outside, you need to take care of the inside. Condensation will still happen but moisture can be absorbed by installing a portable dehumidifier. We DO NOT recommend the disposable products out there as most people forget to empty them. Once they're full of water they can either spill or evaporate, in which case the chemicals used to absorb the water will put a film of caustic residue on your tack and tack room walls. We do recommend the Eva-Dry 500 or the similar Remington model for around $25. These are rechargeable, good for up to 500 sq ft and last for years. In extremely wet tack rooms or LQ areas, a small portable fan will help with air circulation.

With living quarters trailers and for those with water tanks, it's important to have all the water drained out and any lines, including the P-traps, blown free of moisture so it won't get trapped and freeze. It never hurts to pour in some RV antifreeze just as precautionary measure. Don't forget the horse water tanks need to be drained and sterilized with ¼ cup of bleach. In the spring, sterilize the tank again, rinse and drain before refilling.

Chapter 13

Upgrading and customizing horse trailers

Living luxuriously in small spaces

Everyone loves luxury. If you are traveling with your horse, having a comfortable place to sleep after riding becomes especially important. Bunking down in a tent or your trailer's tack room has limitations, and you may soon yearn for the accoutrements of living quarters (LQ) trailers. However, LQs are expensive, and unless you travel frequently and have a tow vehicle capable of hauling them, they may not be a good financial or time investment as they require the same maintenance as an RV.

If you aren't into tenting, but would still like to have a few conveniences, there are many simple, less expensive options available, which you can add as needed or as budget allows. This also gives you the option to remove some of them for use elsewhere. Portable generators are a good example.

Bedding down

If you have a spacious tack room, lightweight foldaway cots can be added. Obviously you can also use them in the stall area of the trailer, depending on whether the trailer is completely enclosed so as not to allow rain to get in. If you're sleeping in your tack room, make certain you have adequate ventilation and an interior safety latch in place for added security.

Tack rooms that don't have enough floor space can have drop down bunks installed on the long headwall. The bed needs to be anchored safely into the structural framework or you may have a nasty surprise if it rips away during the night. Anchoring into framework also prevents damage to the trailer wall.

Showering

Hot water units that work off an auxiliary propane tank, with water supplied from the unit upon demand, can be used in the stall area after the horses are unloaded. These are quite portable and can be used for other applications, such as washing your horse. Of course, if you have wood floors, this will increase the amount of moisture filtering down below the rubber mats and onto the wood. If you use a stall shower frequently, remember to remove your mats just as often to allow the wood floors to dry thoroughly. To prevent damage to wood floors, portable outdoor shower enclosures are a good alternative, and easy to set up.

Electricity (Auxiliary batteries and generators)

Auxiliary batteries can be added, but not combined with, the emergency breakaway system. You will need a charging unit to keep the auxiliary battery fully charged, which can work off either your tow vehicle or shore power (meaning from your house or other AC plug in). It's preferable to install auxiliary batteries externally, or in an enclosure vented to the outside, as they do give off certain toxic gases as they charge. They're not advisable for a small, confined space.

When purchasing a battery charger ensure that it has an automatic shutoff so as not to overcharge the installed battery. It's preferable to use a deep cycle battery that is made specifically for that application, such as a Group 27 size. Battery chargers with the automatic shutoff should be marine grade and water resistant to avoid corrosion and potential failure.

It's a good idea to enclose the charger and the auxiliary battery system in its own housing, such as a box, to protect it from dust and debris or being bumped by tack. Also make sure that once you are at your camp site, if you're equipped with an auxiliary battery that is charged off the vehicle, that you disconnect the cord end that plugs in from the tow vehicle so as not to draw down the tow vehicle battery, as this will prevent the tow vehicle from starting.

Some trailers interior lights are wired differently and may only function when plugged into the tow vehicle. It's imperative that your lighting system gets properly, professionally wired into the auxiliary system with fuse protection to avoid problems.

Lighting

LED lighting is preferable as it provides a great deal of light and uses milliamps rather than amps, which will draw down the battery faster. The only drawback is that they're two to three times the price, depending on quality, but well worth the upgrade expense, both inside and out. You can also purchase inexpensive portable LED lights with magnetic backs or hooks (for use in aluminum trailers) at hardware stores. These can be used inside the trailer in dark areas. You can use them for additional lighting outdoors as well, just remove them before you drive off as you may lose them traveling over bumpy roads.

Refrigerators

Small 3-way refrigerators are heavy (and expensive) and may not stand up well to the bouncing of the trailer. A lightweight alternative is to get a portable cooler with the flexibility to be used either hot or cold. Coleman sells a Thermoelectric cooler (40 qt) that retails for around $150 with the adapter. It will keep foods up to 40 F colder or hotter, depending on outside temperatures but you would need an auxiliary battery to run it.

A simple trick to conserve your battery power for this type of unit is to put in a bag of ice, which will keep the unit cooler and not have to run as much or draw down the battery to keep things at a cool temperature.

Heating

Portable propane heaters (such as Mr. Heater) are extremely efficient and have safety devices such as tip over switches that shut them down if they're knocked over. Keep in mind that when using them in a tack room or stall area, you're in a very small space that doesn't require a great deal of heat to bring up the temperature. These devices do use oxygen to keep the elements burning so proper ventilation is imperative when you're in a small confined space.

Ventilation and safety measures

Trailers and their tack rooms should have adequate ventilation. Not only is this healthier for the horses and riders, it also helps decrease odors and prevent mold. However, venting air in as well as out also allows moisture to get in, so a portable dehumidifier is essential. You also need a propane sniffing device to detect leaks, which should be installed 6" off the floor (propane is heavier than air) and are inexpensive.

At the sleeping level, carry a CO2 sensor, so if the air is inadequate for human breathing it will set off an alarm to warn you. If used properly, and with proper ventilation, they will keep you safe. Most are battery powered, so make sure the batteries are always good. They are also portable so you can use them for other applications.

One of the most essential items to carry in your tack room is a large fire extinguisher. It must be ABC rated, which covers all conditions and uses. Needless to say, you should also have a couple of ABC rated fire extinguishers in your barn, especially near hay and grain.

Water tanks

There are many water tank options, such as vertical triangular tanks that utilize the unused corner space in your tack room. You can also get water tanks for your truck bed or ones that have a brush tray and bench built into the top. It is important that you have a drip tray underneath water tanks so as not to soak carpets or rot out wood floors. Water tanks will also increase condensation in a small area so that's another reason to carry a portable dehumidifier.

Sanitize water tanks on a semi annual basis, both potable (fresh) water and your horse's water. A commercial sanitizing product or even Clorox is good, and will kill most bacteria, but use it to manufacturers' specifications. Be sure to rinse the system thoroughly to remove the sanitizer and supply fresh clean water.

Sinks

A simple bar sink with a 12 Volt battery, powered on demand (only comes on when you need it) and a five gallon water container, plumbed properly, will provide more than enough potable water for personal use.

This is easy to maintain, and there is no weatherizing as it requires just removing the water container. It will save a lot of money in time and maintenance and uses very little power. This will give you the same results as an LQ that has permanent water tanks and extra wiring.

The teak wet bar shown on the next page was custom fitted into the unused corner area of a gooseneck trailer.

Toilets

A portable flushable toilet, many for $100 or less, is one of the most useful items to carry in your trailer. Make sure you follow instructions for safe waste handling and disposal. Never dump waste on the ground. In addition to this being extremely unsanitary and bad for the environment, it can also result in a hefty fine.

Appliances

Technology has advanced greatly. Inverters, properly and professionally installed, will change battery power to household current (AC) and run appliances that you normally use in your home. The appliances you're intending to use, such as microwaves and refrigerators, will need the proper auxiliary power via the batteries to run this type of technology, i.e., inverters. Portable generators have come a long way and have become more inexpensive (some for around $200) and are capable of not only providing AC power to certain appliances but also DC power or a charge unit that will maintain your auxiliary power DC system (batteries). They are quiet and easy to transport.

Unless you have a certain sized battery bank, such as dual batteries, AC wired appliances will draw down the battery power substantially, unless you're conservative about their use. You can buy relatively inexpensive appliances (such as blenders, blow dryers, etc.) that run off of DC power. Consult a professional with any technical questions about their use.

Customizing for equine safety and comfort

When horses are unhappy in a trailer or refuse to load, the problem (and solution) may be found in the trailer itself.

- Is the horse too confined (i.e., not enough room from nose to tail)?

- Does he prefer a straight load to a slant, or vice versa?
- Does he constantly have to correct his balance in a slant?

Once you are able to narrow down WHY the horse is unhappy with being in a trailer (no small task), you can work on the remedy. Slant loads can be modified into a straight load, but to turn a straight load into a slant the straight load would need to be a minimum width of 7 feet. As most straight loads are much narrower than this, your only option would be to remove the center divider to give the horse more room and haul him alone. In addition, most straight loads would not have enough stall length to accommodate a second horse standing on a slant.

Often the reason that a horse is unhappy being hauled has more to do with the owner's towing habits and abilities than the trailer itself, i.e., fast starts, stops and turns, which makes it difficult for the horse to retain his balance. **You** can see and compensate for where you're going, but your horse in the trailer cannot anticipate turns or stops.

Corral panels

Corral panels can be mounted on the exterior passenger side of the trailer. But not all panels and mounts will fit all trailers. Before purchasing, careful measurements should be taken so the mounting brackets do not encumber the tack room door. It's important to mount them into the structural support of the trailer or severe damage to the exterior walls will result.

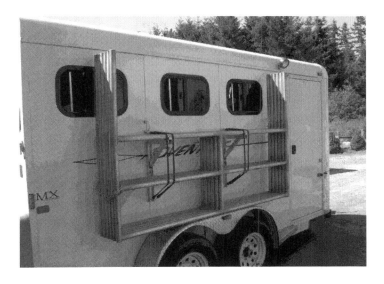

The photos on the next page show custom remodeling on a stock/slant trailer with no center divider. It was modified into a straight load as it was too narrow on the diagonal to accommodate horses. An articulated, removable divider was added that collapses the center against the headwall. The divider is also removable for versatility. The tack room was left intact.

Other accessories that can be added:

- solar panels to maintain battery levels (break-away battery can be wired into solar)
- security devices or alarms
- portable air conditioners
- stall area cameras for hauling

Remember that everything you add to your trailer will increase its weight. If you have added a number of accoutrements, you should have your loaded trailer weighed to see if it exceeds your gross vehicle weight rating (GVWR) of not only the tow vehicle but the trailer itself. If it does, this will stress all the major working components on your trailer and wear them out prematurely.

It is also important that your tow vehicle have the sufficient GVWR for towing such a weight, which might result in a ticket if you are overloaded.

Therefore, it's better to start gradually, adding the most important items first.

One last tip: read lots of reviews before purchasing portable items. Going with a cheap item rather than a name brand with a good warranty may not save you money in the long run.

Chapter 14

Troubleshooting
and emergencies

Necessities to have
when towing

Useful tips

A ramp needs to be on an even level surface when the horse is on it, otherwise it will bow out of alignment and possibly break a hinge. If you have a trailer with a ramp, be sure to carry a couple of foot long 2x4's to support it and compensate for the uneven ground.

All trailers should be kept as dry as possible, not only to make them last longer, but to keep tack and carpeted areas free from mold and mildew. We recommend using a small battery operated or electric fan and a dehumidifier.

If your trailer lights and brakes are not coming on, check to see if the cord end connecter is corroded. If it is, use an emery board (not a nail file—metal is a conductor!) to gently remove and clean the green corrosion. Rubbing alcohol with a toothpick is also useful to clean it and then you can use the emery board. Keep in mind not to use any metallic cleaning tool, especially if you have an auxiliary battery which could give you a nasty shock.

Avoid using grease when lubricating the ball hitch, as this will only get all over your hands and clothes. Do not use WD-40, which is a solvent, not a lubricant. Instead use a dry Lithium-based aerosol lubricant, which goes on wet and dries, prevents friction and build-up and allows metal shavings to fall out.

Trailer mats can be moved quite easily. Fold the mats away from you over a long lead rope, then taking each end of the rope and pulling upward and toward you.

SAFETY AND PREVENTATIVE MAINTENANCE

Pre-trip check

☐ Check tires for proper inflation, weather cracks and uneven wear.

☐ Inspect all trailer tires (including spares) for signs of heat checking or cracks, correct air pressure, faulty air valves, uneven tire wear, overall tire wear, and damage. Use a high-quality air pressure gauge to inspect tire pressure before each trip. Tires need a minimum amount of 1/4" of tread. Replace tires if worn or damaged. Tires should be replaced every three to five years regardless of mileage. When replacing tires, always replace the valve stems. Only high quality tires specifically designed and weight rated for trailers should be used. Never use retread or automobile tires on a horse trailer.

☐ Inspect brakes and emergency breakaway cable, pin and control box, and battery.

☐ Make sure lights and reflectors are working.

☐ Inspect flooring inside the trailer for cracks and rotted areas.

☐ Check interior for wasps and bees.

☐ Program emergency contact information into your cell phone under the listing designation "ICE," which stands for In Case of Emergency.

HAULING YOUR HORSE

- Distribute your load weight, use of torsion bars or load leveling system is recommended. Do NOT overload beyond GVWR capacity.

- If hauling fewer horses in a trailer that has the capacity for more, space them out to even the load. Have sufficient tongue weight forward.

- If you get into a tight spot, do not brake suddenly unless absolutely necessary.

- Gauge your speed to the road, weather and traffic conditions. Allow for three lengths of your tow vehicle and trailer for ten mph. Always travel in the right lane, which is the law in most states.

- In the case of bad weather, sleepiness or known problems ahead, pull into a safe area and wait it out. Being in a hurry to get somewhere could cost you your life!

STOCK YOUR TRAILER WITH
PERMANENT ESSENTIALS

☐   Human first aid kit

☐   Emergency contact numbers for you and your horse, in a Ziploc bag (so they can be easily seen) on a tack room wall of your trailer.

☐   Certificate of Veterinary Inspection (Health Certificate) dated within 30 days

☐   Proof of negative EIA (Coggins) usually dated within 1 year. Some states are 6 months.

☐   Certificate of Brand Inspection if applicable

☐   Spare Tire/Jack/Tire Iron

☐   Three emergency triangles or flares (triangles are preferred)

☐   Chocks (four). Rubber, not plastic.

☐   Flashlight (with new batteries)

☐   Electrical tape and Duct tape

☐   Equine first aid kit with splint, Banamine, Bute and tranquilizer

☐   Knife for cutting ropes, etc., in emergency

☐   Water and water hose

☐   Buckets/sponge

☐   Blanket for your horse in case he goes into shock

☐   Spare halter and lead rope for each horse

☐   Spare bulbs for exterior and interior lights

☐   Spare fuses if applicable

☐   Fire extinguisher with up to date inspection and fully charged (ABC rated)

☐   Dry Lithium or other lubricant, like 3-in-1 oil

☐   Broom, shovel, fork, manure disposal bags

☐ Insect spray (bee and wasp). Never spray with the horse inside. After spraying, air it out for at least an hour before hauling livestock. Never spray where residue will come in contact with animals.

In the Tow Vehicle

☐ Registration for the vehicle and trailer
☐ Proof of insurance on both
☐ Jumper cables
☐ Spare tire/jack/tire iron
☐ Tool kit including wiring materials
☐ Spare belts and hoses for the tow vehicle
☐ Tow chain or strap
☐ Cellular phone (with ICE names logged in)
☐ Charger for cell and/or CB radio for areas without cell phone signals
☐ GPS, maps or road atlas
☐ Replacement fuses
☐ Work gloves, rain gear with reflective tape, blanket
☐ Emergency drinking water for humans and animals, nonperishable food supplies
☐ Portable air compressor or can of Fix-a-flat
☐ Extra cash/credit card
☐ Equine emergency guide
☐ AAA* or USRider contact information for emergency towing
  * AAA will not tow trailers with animals in, however, USRider may

Check your inventory frequently and replace used or removed items before each trip **Keep all the above readily accessible in case of emergency!**

MAINTAINING YOUR TRAILER

Regular maintenance check

☐ Examine floor boards for cracks, rot or sagging (top side and underneath)

☐ Check tires for wear

☐ Check spare tire for safety

☐ Jacks and safety triangles or reflectors should be in good working order in case of breakdown. (Ignitable flares should not be stored in the horse trailer because of fire potential)

☐ Replace any boards that are questionable. To help lengthen the life of a trailer floor, mats should be removed after use and the floor swept or hosed out. If the floor is hosed be sure it is dry before the mats are replaced. Yearly applications of a weather sealer on the floor boards will also extend their life.

☐ Any screws, bolts or nails that may have worked loose and are protruding from the inside of the trailer should be removed, or tightened and replaced.

☐ All lights (marker, tail, brake, directional and interior) should be working and bright.

☐ Hitch welds, safety chain welds and snaps should be in good repair.

☐ Wheel chocks should be in good condition and used anytime the trailer is unhitched.

Yearly maintenance check
(It is advisable to have a licensed professional perform these checks.)

☐ Inspection of frame and suspension for cracks

☐ Inspect wires for loose connections and frayed covering

☐ Repair or replacement of rotted or rusted metal

☐ Lubricate all hinges, springs, etc.

☐ Inspection of ramp hinges and springs for weakness and cracks

☐ Wheels should be pulled and bearings inspected and repacked, if needed, on an annual basis (regardless of mileage) due to moisture build-up. Keep a spare set of wheel bearings in your trailer in case of premature failure

☐ Inspect trailer wiring and lighting; inspect door latches and lubricate the doors; inspect the floor (remove any rubber mats so the entire floor can be examined); and inspect and lubricate mechanical moving parts

☐ If the trailer has been sitting for a while, check for wasp nests and other insects.

Traveling tips

- Always plan your trips well in advance.
- Know the terrain you're traveling.
- Belonging to a national equestrian group is to your advantage in case of an emergency. Be prepared to reciprocate if they are in your location.
- Carry two spares.
- Carry emergency cash.
- Map emergency boarding facilities for your horse along the way.
- Check out reputable repair and vet facilities along the route. Program their contact info into your cell phone, and their availability, i.e., after hours.
- Travel in groups, if possible, or with a friend.
- Make others aware of your route and timeline.
- Carry spare sets of keys to tow vehicle and trailer.
- Check with your insurance company to know emergency service coverage prior to needing it.
- Carry this Owner's Manual with your tow vehicle at all times.
- When in doubt, don't go.

CHECKSLIST FOR BUYING
A USED TRAILER

What to check for when buying a used trailer

- Rust: with both interior or exterior rusting, is it just surface rust, or all the way through

- Bulging seams or split framework from poor moisture drainage

- Look under rubber mats for damaged floorboards

- Are all lights working or in place, including reflectors

- Rusting on framework underneath floorboards

- Check all welds, especially on doors and framework

- Check roof for rust, dried out caulking

- Check undercarriage for structural damage and underside of floorboards

- Worn out tires

Don't forget: Before making an offer on a trailer, ask to take the trailer to a trusted, qualified trailer mechanic to perform a safety inspection on all systems to ensure they're in proper working order.

ABOUT THE AUTHOR

Leigh Goodison Grieve's articles, essays, short stories and poetry have appeared in publications across North America since 1980. She currently lives on five acres in Battle Ground, Washington, with her beloved dog, Xena, four Arabian horses, seven cats, and her partner and co-owner of Horse Trailer Restoration, LLC, David Bodin, and his son, Sidney.

If you enjoyed this book and would like more information on horse trailers, you may wish to purchase our DVDs:

Horse Trailers: 101
Horse Trailer Repair & Maintenance
Horse Trailer Upgrading & Customizing
Horse Trailer Troubleshooting & Emergencies
Buying a Horse Trailer

To order, visit: www.handyrider.com/shopping

Sheffield Publications
www.sheffieldpublications.com

16532744R00075

Made in the USA
Charleston, SC
26 December 2012